Strategic Implementation of mobileGovernment: core principles

Ibrahim Kushchu

mobileGov UK's
Series on mGovernment: Vol III

November 2016

ISBN: 978-1-912037-71-1
ISBN-13: 978-1912037711

DEDICATION

To all those who believe in the power of sharing knowledge ...

About mobileGov UK's Series on Mobile Government:

Over the years mobileGov UK has accumulated significant resources in the form of articles, reports, training materials and presentations, mostly produced in house and gathered from actual projects completed. The aim of these series is to share this accumulated knowledge via series of volumes each of which contains essential information on transition to mobileGovernment and modernizing the public sector organizations.

Please also see other volumes in 'mobileGov UK's Series on mGovernment:' each of which focuses one fundamental topic in adopting and implementing mobileGovernment. In this way a good collection of essential information on mGovernment related topics will be compiled.

This Particular Volume in Your Hand is a reflection of recent trend in approaches to mobileGovernment. Many countries now consider mobile government as their primary IT agenda in eGovernment and would like to strategically design and implement it. This volume, developed from actual project work, is a comprehensive presentation of strategic mobile government that can guide central government activities in this matter.

ACKNOWLEDGMENTS

The field of mobileGovernment as a practice has been growing significantly and implemented successfully by various governments since our early efforts from early 2000s by valuable contributions of my students in Japan, colleagues and many professionals from all around the world, all of whom, deserve gratitude and appreciation. Thanks to all wholeheartedly.

Special thanks to the team at the mobileGov UK. Without their encouragement, hard work and efforts none of these volumes would be produced
.

CONTENTS

1. The Context for mGovernment

The history work on mGovernment is short compared with eGovernment efforts that has been around for sometime. As capabilities of mobile technologies and relevant infrastructure advance, new opportunities attracts all kinds of organizations including that of public sector with aim of benefiting from these. Despite a reasonably well acceptance of significance of mobile technologies for offering services to citizens and for modernizing government operations, the place, meaning and functionalities of mGovernment is not well understood. Before discussing various issues related to strategic mGovernment adoption and implementation, it is important to clarify the context in which mGovernment lives. This section makes an effort to clarify such context by explaining the relationship between eGovernment and mGovernment, various perspectives on the views of mGovernment, and the goals and outcomes of the mGovernment. In this way, this section forms a basis for further technical issues that are related understanding implementing mGovernment strategically.

The structure of this section is as follows. The next section of this chapter briefly describes the concepts of eGovernment and mGovernment and how they are interrelated. The second section contains an analysis of the perspectives on mGovernment and further investigates its implications for local and central government levels as well as the citizens' point of view. Additionally, the structural perspective is followed up raising the impacts of demographic and political structure of a country on mGovernment. The third section, the goals and the expected outcomes of a successful mGovernment implementation are presented. Finally, the structure of this document will be laid out before detailing important strategic issues.

1.1.-eGovernment and mGovernment: How Do They Relate?

eGovernment has been a big revolution in understanding how governments operate at the central and local levels and how they interact with citizens over more than two decades now around the world. eGovernment projects aimed to transform existing traditional government structure into a model that makes use of the information and communication technologies (ICT) in every aspect of the public service.[i] Primarily, eGovernment is designed to enhance the quality and efficiency of the interaction among government departments as well as citizens and businesses. It has profoundly changed the workflow within government entities and the way they interact with citizens and businesses although the level of maturity varied among the countries implementing eGovernment.

Several countries sustained a good level of 'connected government' where government organizations share back-end data and manage the use raw data to create valuable information for citizens, for policy decision-making and for the use of governmental records albeit in varying degrees of maturity. Establishing a secure Intranet between government organizations played a key enabling role for data and information sharing along with increased government-wide workflow efficiency. Citizens and businesses have also benefited from transformed workflows within the government as availability of online services reduced efforts and time spent on bureaucratic procedures to handle government interactions.

However, there are certain limitations to eGovernment some caused by digital divide, digital literacy and accessibility and some casued by various factors including effective use of technological offerings, instability, political support, etc., which all constituted some sort of setbacks of eGovernment.[ii] Effectively, this is where mGovernment comes to rescue.

In general terms, the idea of mGovernment is to make use of mobile technologies in order to offer better services and interaction experience to citizens at *anytime* and *anywhere* while modernizing the public sector operations with newest technologies. As a definition, mGovernment is a "strategy and its implementation involving the utilization of all kinds of wireless and mobile technology, services, applications and devices for improving benefits to the parties involved in e-government including citizens, businesses and all government units".[iii]

mGovernment is the natural next step after eGovernment. Some consider it as a domain within eGovernment since the idea of mGovernment emerged through eGovernment developments in the world. Some considers it just a new way of channeling services. It really does not matter much. What is known is that it supplements the eGovernment and augments it in new possible ways by the unique features of mobile technologies. Just as eGovernment transformed business processes, workflows and interactions with citizens; mobile government services also are playing a transformative role in public administration in parallel to requirements of adopting mobile technologies in public organisations.[iv] The conventional e-government efforts provide services through wired network with interactive and relatively intelligent network applications. The value of mGovernment comes from the new and innovative capabilities of applications supporting mobility of the citizens, businesses, and in parallel, the required transformation of internal operations of the governments, at a central and local level.

Therefore the relationship between eGovernment and mGovernment should be seen as advances in government operations and services offered via opportunities brought by mobile technologies rather than a simple classification or a competitive comparison between the two.

1.2 Different Perspectives of mGovernment

A good understanding of mGovernment is closely related to from which perspective it is being viewed. This has implications for successful implementation. In some cases, it may be viewed as an effective way in offering services to citizens while having a great impact on public sector transformations. mGovernment implementation may be a big task for a total central government operations, but many local government organizations may find it easier to implement. Then comes the structure and organization of the government, whether it is centralized or not, and how the government agencies are distributed and managed within a country, which may influence considerations towards mGovernment. Also important are demographics such as population, level of income and education, which all may have influence on how mGovernment may be understood too. In the following sections such perspectives on mGovernment will be evaluated.

1.2.1. Citizen Faced or Public Sector Transformation Oriented

mGovernment has implications both on improving the public sector operations internally and on the citizen front to offer better services. Some of the mGovernment services are designed with a citizen-oriented approach to provide them anywhere and anytime public services in their own convenience for the sole purpose of citizen satisfaction and happiness. There are other mGovernment service deployments, however, that aims to transform the internal operation of the government entities or that are designed for government employees or field workers targeting more efficient processes and more integrated workflow among the institutions. These two views of mGovernment are very much interrelated. For instance, creating citizen oriented mobile services impacts the organizational workflow of government institutions that may result in reduction in visits to government offices by citizens. This may event result in redundant work and workflows. Similarly, there are pressures on government organizations for mobile technology adoption that are aimed for transforming internal operations of government agencies to make them more effective and effcient. These ultimately prove to be beneficial to citizens such as healthcare benefits due to an integrated medical database of patients, field worker services benefitting elderly in daily care and at home, etc.

Therefore, doption of mobile technologies by government units not only benefits the parties who use these services, but also can have a positive impact on the internal workings of public sector organizations. At a first glance, applying wireless technologies within traditionally bureaucratic, slow-paced and rigid public sector entities may seem a little out of place. However, the increasing number of mobile government applications around the world shows that there are many opportunities for governments to improve and enhance their services and cut down on operational costs to enhance organizational effectiveness. Traffic navigation assistance, emergency assistance, weather updates, notification for tax and bill payments, field inspections, and tracking systems for stolen vehicles are some of the more common applications used by the public sector that fall into this class.

Introduction of mobile technologies in public sector can result in:
- Establishment of new virtual departments
- Flatter organization, enhanced knowledge sharing
- Better data keeping, storing and processing procedures
- More efficient processes by gathering, updating and processing data from all departments anytime and anywhere
- Training for new skills, new job descriptions
- Flexible working environment[v]

Coming back to being citizen oriented as another perspective, one may just observe that mGovernment services are ultimately designed for citizen satisfaction and happiness. Citizen oriented governments are characterized and evaluated by their front-end services that answer citizens' requirement on any given occasion. Focusing merely on how to provide citizens a better, more inclusive, more efficient and more convenient services, citizen oriented mGovernment can be characterized by openness, transparency and collaboration. Citizen centricity implies government's dedication to meet citizen's expectations and exceeding it when possible in order to achieve high standards of government services. It may impose being open and transparent regarding upcoming plans and projects and engaging citizens into decision-making procedures and have their participation in possible stages of service innovation and implementation. Citizen centricity also involves agencies' readiness to serve citizens needs anytime anywhere and by any means. Therefore, citizen oriented mGovernment projects normally should focus on being always accessible, providing all relevant key information, maintaining seamless interaction and making transactions on the go.

It is then important to understand that there are actually two distinct perspectives on mGovernment one being citizen oriented and the other focusing on improving internal operations especially for those government workers performing outside the offices. There are certain mGovernment services that solely focus on improving operations of public sector organizations such as inspection and emergency services. However, it is strategically important to have deeper understanding of how these operations may strengthen the overall operations of relevant government units and as a result also provide better services to citizens. Similarly, it is important to significantly understand that citizen centric operations are not simply oriented to offer better experiences to the citizens but they also have great impact on the internal structure and workflow of the public sector organizations.

1.2.2. Local vs. Central

mGovernment implementation may have different implications for the local government operations and central government (i.e. ministries) activities. These differences are stemming mainly from the way central and local governments operate, their day-to-day proximity to the general public and the nature of their authority and responsibilities. Central government bodies are often operate internally within a top down structure to organize and regulate government activities, whereas local government units may be seen as having more direct citizen facing activities. Central government by its very nature is the planning, decision and policy making authority, while local governments are more practically involved in day-to-day implementation of policies and projects. And as such are more closer to citizens.

In the context of mGovernment, these differences may be the defining elements of the role that central and local governments play. Essentially, mGovernment strategy of a country needs to be centrally put forward yet there are aspects of mGovernment implementation in which local governments and central governments need to act in their own way.[vi]

At central level the focus may primarily be concerned with planning and regulating the mGovernment development and implementations. Central governments also play key role in nationwide deployments, such as data management, central data infrastructure implementation and management, nationwide mobile platform payment facility, secure electronic identity services, mobile health services, disaster management services and highway traffic management systems. The common denominator of all these key services is that it exceeds the borders of local governments' authority and responsibilities. This is the reason why the deployment of country-wide services require effective involvement of central government bodies. Financial, legal, organizational and infrastructural decisions relevant to mGovernment implementations may also be arranged centrally.[vii]

Local governments, however, have a different context. They may be local independent government bodies such as municipalities or may be local representation (agencies) of central government organisations. In either case, they are generally in the heart of the most visible mGovernment services since their operations are in more proximity to citizens' day to day actions. They have the opportunity to create services according to the particuliar requirements of their local context and are able to respond to citizens' demands with a degree of independence. For instance, each municipality may independently offer its own urban traffic information services, local notification services, tourist guide and other location based services as well as citizen participation platforms, etc.

Having different views on mGovernment implementations from local or central perspectives is also strategically important. For example, local independent government bodies such as municipalities often need to implement similar services for the citizens. In this case, repetitions need to be avoided. Similarly, planning and policies imposed centrally need to consider the particular situation and context their local representations are operating when developing services. In some cases, especially when the country is geographically and in terms of population size is very large, it may be better to decentralize the mGovernment implementation if it is appropriate for the coutry.

1.2.3. Structural Perspectives on mGovernment

Strategic implementation of mGovernment is also influenced by various factors referring to structure of government and demographics of the country.

The structure of the government perhaps is one of the primary influencing factors of understanding and implementing mGovernment. How is the government organized? Is it a federal system or not? How is the local representation of central or federal government organizations distributed around the country? The tructure of the government inevitably determines how planning and implementation of mGovernment would be conducted in that country.

Other influencing factors include the size and demographics of the population. Often smaller the size and population of the country, the easier it is to understand the requirements of mGovernment. Good examples include the success in implementing mGovernment in Korea, Singapore, Estonia and the UAE. Also important are the percentage of youth, ICT literacy and underserved communities. In Afghanistan around 80 percent of the population does not know hos to read and write and the country is yet to implement mGovernment. How difficult a task it is?

The implementers understanding these structural views may have an easier task and can be more successful in making adoption and implementation of mGovernment for a particular country.

1.3. Goals and Outcomes of mGovernment

The ultimate goal of both eGovernment and mGovernment is to have a 'no government'. This ambitious goal means that the government should operate in such a seamless way that the citizens should be served to the maximum convenience as if there is no need to be in touch with any government offices. While eGovernment in its current level and quality of implementations is far from this goal, mGovernment, with the capabilities mobile technologies, location based services, machine-to-machine communication and intelligent applications, perhaps led by developments in Internet of Things (IoT), is making it more possible to get closer to this goal.

Government entities and employees, citizens and businesses are all beneficiaries of mGovernment. A successful implementation of mGovernment will bring in new operational dimensions to government organizations by transforming the workflows within as well as the style of the cooperation between government agencies at a central or local level. mGovernment can significantly enhance the integrity of government institutions by an integrated back-office infrastructure and empowering government employees with mobile technologies. Business processes gain unprecedented efficiency with the internal transformation of government operations. Despite the initial implementation costs of technological infrastructure, mGovernment solutions prove to be decreasing costs drastically, adding financial gains on top of the efficiency gains.[viii]

Governments have a great opportunity to expand their reach to citizens through mobile technology[ix] by offering them services on the go. Rather than limiting the public services within (office) time and place (government offices, hospitals etc.), central and local governments are motivated to be accessible all the time and serve the requirements of citizens anytime and anywhere.

mGovernment presents various benefits for citizens as they are the ultimate targets in mGovernment ecosystem to be served. Among others, citizens can have access to up-to-date strategic information, have a say on local decisions, file complaints with image and video support right from the spot, vote in public surveys and even reach out to governors to share opinion on matters that they relate to.[x] Paying for parking tickets, receiving notifications of choice, getting mobile transport tickets, carrying own medical history to the hospital on a mobile device and finding out train schedules are, hence, becoming the new norm in ordinary people's lives and the amount of time and effort to interact with government is getting less and less with such services.[xi]

Besides, business sector has a lot to gain owing to the developments in mGovernment. Mobile network operators, service providers, software designers, financial institutions, technology providers, device manufacturers and a list of other stakeholders are directly subject to market improvements resulting from flourishing markets due to mGovernment.

mGovernment, therefore, is bringing in benefits to the private and public sector organisations and significantly better conveniences to citizens owing to the developments and the use of mobile technologies. Further, there are already considerable evidences how mobile intelligent systems drastically remove the need for the citizens to interact with government offices. The outcome of implementing mGovernment result in various benefits to the governments, businesses and citizens and makes us closer to the ideal state of having a 'no government'.

1.4 Structure of The Remaining Material

In the current chapter, an overview with a context and various perspectives is presented in order to clarify and promote a better understanding of approaches to mGovernment. The following chapter describes the mGovernment ecosystem and the key actors in the mobile value chain, which has implications on issues related to a strategic implementation. Then the third chapter discusses why a strategic vision is essential to implement mGovernment in a given country. Fourth chapter presents a number of critical prerequisites of mGovernment before implementation. The following chapter, chapter fifth, elaborates on essential steps involved in successful mGovernment implementation. Sixth chapter introduces several key enablers of mobile services such as mobileID, Trusted Service Manager (TSM) and mPayment systems. Seventh chapter investigates the advantages of promoting innovation and the critical role of pilot projects for a thriving mGovernment environment. Finally, chapter eight discusses the opportunities to attain high levels of mobile services adoption and argues that mGovernment implementation is a continuous process and governments should always keep in track with the latest trends in mobile technologies to the extend possible.

2. mGovernment Ecosystem and Stakeholders

mGovernment ecosystem involves several key stakeholders in addition to the government institutions. Implementing mGovernment projects requires contribution and commitment not only from government and its employees, but also from different market actors in mobile value chain and from the citizens themselves. Success of these implementations depends largely on the adequacy of these stakeholders and the synergy of the collaboration between them. Each one of these stakeholders offers unique contributions to mobile government ecosystem and has its own benefits from it.

Governments often have a difficult task to sustain productive relationship among involved stakeholders, and at the same time, implement strategies to empower weak stakeholder groups or enable a productive environment for them. It may be because of this difficulty the significance and potential benefits of working with stakeholders are often not given sufficient care that they deserve. Succeeding in a coordinated partnerships with key stakeholders will greatly contribute to the success of mGovernment implementation and therefore it is important to understand who they are and what their roles may be.

As depicted in the Figure below, mGovernment ecosystem has three groups of stakeholders: *Service Providers, Mobile ICT Industry and Users.* The first set, service providers are those that provide services on mobile platform to the end users. Governments are the main service providers within mGovernment ecosystem. However, banks and financial institutions as well as third party (Trusted Services Management) TSMs are also critical service providers for the end users. The second group constitutes the mobile ICT sector as a key component of the mGovernment ecosystem, which often found to be mediating these services to end-users. Mobile Network Operators (MNOs) are very central to making various mobile services be available. Device manufacturers, content and service developers support the technical side of the operations relevant to developing mServices. The ultimate beneficiary as a stakeholder in this ecosystem is the user. Users are at the receiving end of the provided services including the citizens, businesses, NGOs, government entities and employees. They also put pressures to government organizations to come up and deliver high quality services.

2.1. Key Actors in mGovernment

Below is the analysis of the stakeholders in mobile government ecosystem that have crucial roles in creating an environment where mGovernment can flourish to the extent that mutual partnerships and collaboration can be established among them.

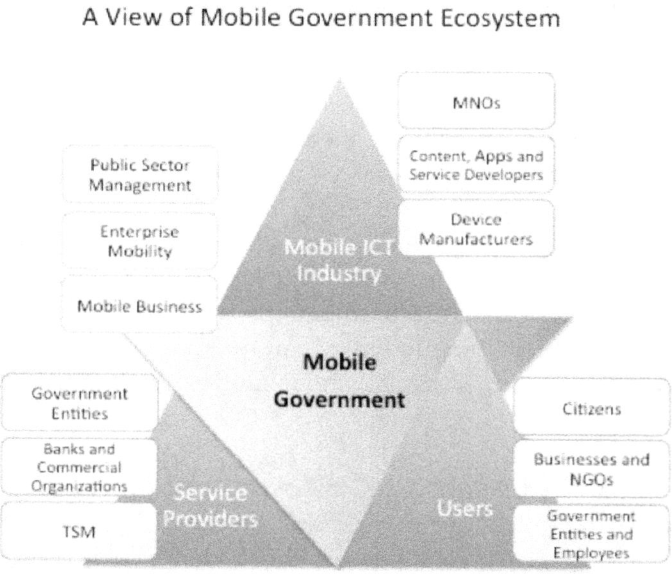

A View of Mobile Government Ecosystem

Figure 1 mGovernment Ecosystem

Service Providers: Governments are clearly in the focal point of mGovernment ecosystem and are the main stakeholder that shapes the characteristics of the entire implementation. Governments design the general strategy and targets of mGovernment services. They lead the think-tank of the entire business with variety of partnerships and may greatly influence the formation of the initial idea of the most suitable mGovernment for the country. In order to move towards the target, governments rearrange policies and regulations and develop standards for different segments of the mGovernment architecture.

Governments play the most active role in the ecosystem through organizing. Quite a number of activities are inlved: research and development (R&D) for resources, making decisions on technology choices, planning capacity building for government employees and citizens, setting up close relationships with the mobile market to drive innovation, building infrastructure, engaging citizens in mGovernment services creation and design, and always checking the accomplishments, assessing them.

Besides the governments as the leading central service provider in the ecosystem, there are also banks and other financial institutions as well as Trusted Services Management (TSM) units that provide security and confidentiality of key mobile services. Many transactional services require financial institutions and trusted third parties to be involved in order to secure and manage the transactions when users are paying for services.

Mobile ICT Industry: There are various actors in mobile value chain that play indispensable roles in mGovernment environment. Among others, MNOs play a key role in mGovernment ecosystem mainly because they hold a very central role in various areas of mobile services.[xii] They provide the intermediary tool to connect service providers with their users. MNOs around the world are engaging their efforts more and more to governmental projects as well as private initiatives undertaken by businesses and NGOs. Almost every new service or application area creates new revenue streams to MNOs. Various types of mGovernment services that use SMS, mobile data, voice channel or other channels create sustainable revenues for MNOs. Moreover, recently MNOs are playing crucial roles in enabling infrastructure implementations by working closely with governments. Therefore, they participate in a more beneficial part of mGovernment business by providing infrastructure and initiating innovative mobile projects. Active participation in planning and implementation of 'enabling mobile services' such as TSMs, Mobile Identity services, national mPayment system and government data center infrastructure are the new trends between MNOs with expectation of having enormous presence in mGovernment ecosystem.[xiii]

One of the other actors, application developers, provides the interface for service delivery from service providers to the end users. End users may be citizens, businesses, government employees and government entities themselves. Applications use device functionalities to connect to the network of the service providers', enabling data flow and transactional activities between them.[xiv]

Application developer's critical role grounds itself on managing how users interact with the service providers. These also include making arrangements for the specific requirements of the services. Personalization of services has a lot to do with the application design and usability and needs to be provided by the developers. Synchronization issues, accessibility concerns, authorization and authentication procedures as well as managing application lifecycles are all part of the application developers' role in mGovernment ecosystem.

Device manufacturers are the producers of mobile devices that enable delivery of mobile services over voice, data, SMS and other related channels.[xv] Devices vary depending on the use cases and the agency that is using it. As for the citizens mobile phones, smart phones and tablets are the devices that mGovernment services could be reached with. There are diverse other devices that are in use in mobile public service delivery varying greatly from health sector to law enforcement, emergency management to field work. Device manufacturers have their crucial task to produce devices for different requirements of the consumers, which differ in functionality, size, quality and quantity.

Users: The ultimate target for every mGovernment service is the satisfaction of the end users and enhancing service quality for them. End users are the citizens, businesses, NGOs and also governments' own entities and employees. Citizens and businesses around the world are generally ahead of their governments in terms of mobile technology adoption and uptake. Therefore, their expectation and benefits in terms of mGovernment revolve around utilizing these technologies in accessing government services on the go with maximum convenience.[xvi] As it was the case with MNOs, however, users of mGovernment services should not be considered as passive consumers of given services. Their role in mGovernment can and should be expanded to being *co-creators or co-producers* of mobile public services. Engagement of citizens and businesses in service creation will benefit all the stakeholders since it will enhance the relevancy and quality of the services and increase the adoption rates significantly.

mGovernment services are emerging to be useful to businesses and NGOs as well. In particular, designed mServices that target certain sectors of businesses from farming to pharmaceutical industry; from trade companies to logistic fleets prove to provide time and cost efficient business processes to users.

Government entities and employees are among the beneficiaries of the mobile platform services themselves. mGovernment services that are used within the public sector internal operations change the way government organizations interact with each other and the way employees work, generally in a positive way. Local and central governments constantly need to expand their capacity in order to increase the quality and efficiency of their services and at the same time optimize the accompanying costs.[xvii] A well-constructed data handling architecture, efficient mobile device and application management may, for instance, reduce duplicate data entry, enhance precise information flow and assist mobile field workers in saving time and travel costs. Intra agency interactions and efficient integration between applications will definitely result in efficient workflow within internal operations. Savings from decreased office visits by citizens also need to be considered among cost reductions due to mobile technology involvement.

3. **Developing an Integrated mGovernment Strategy**

Since the early work of my team at mGovLab in Japan on mGovernment, a number of governments at the local and central level started to adopt mobile technologies as an extension to their existing work in eGovernment. As a result in various countries many notable mGovernment services were developed on the mobile platform but mostly using SMS based services. Similar approaches has been around in some countries where many separate and mostly successful mGovernment solutions are being developed by various government units. This picture shows many islands of mobile government solutions, which are, unfortunately, not coordinated and organized. However recently, the countries are more aware of significance of having mGovernment in their strategic agenda as part of their overall ICT, information society and eGovernment strategy. mobileGov UK recently designed the strategic road maps for Afghanistan and the UAE emphasizing the unavoidable requirements for approaching to mobileGovernment from a strategic viewpoint in the context of all ICT efforts.

A comprehensive mGovernment implementation requires a strategic approach and strategic management. Governments should have a clear vision on the entire setting of mGovernment deployment and mobilize every governmental department and the entire mobile value chain around the same strategic target. Planning and execution should take into account the given context of the country bearing in mind the costs, complexities, and the challenges of the entire project. Integrity should be the main pillar of the overall strategy in order to enable advanced mobile services. Citizen expectation and demand should always be the main motivation of the mGovernment strategy that strives for efficient business processes and citizen happiness. With these in mind, following are the core principles of a "strategic approach" to implement mobileGovernment.

- **Getting all stakeholders put efforts around the same strategy**: Governments and policy makers should consider the requirements of the bigger picture and mobilize resources accordingly. mGovernment transition is a collaborative set of plans and procedures that involve various key stakeholders. Hence, the governing body should have a clear vision of the overall principles of cooperation between key players. MNOs, service providers, device manufacturers, legal and regulatory authorities, all other government entities and newly implemented departments, NGOs and representatives of different communities and, most importantly, citizens should be mobilized under the macro strategy by a strong political will of policy makers and governors.

- **Set achievable targets and plan ahead**: The government entities should guide the mGovernment transformation from the very beginning with formal planning using program and project management techniques. As usual, these plans should be constantly monitored, be flexible and respond to a changing environment, constraints and needs. The planning typically follows core tasks and activities such as the ones suggested in this document and include financing, staffing, technology, advocacy, target citizens and stakeholder involvement and partnerships.

The significance of planning is felt the most as mGovernment pushes the boundaries of the existing work flows and structures into perhaps completely new ways of performing tasks. A successful planning with a long terms success should therefore help to identify key processes, competencies and expected challenges on the way to achieving realistically set goals in transforming the government entity to best accommodate mGovernment implementation.

- **Analyze the local context and its unique requirements**: Policymakers should look into various aspects of mGovernment and consider the unique cases of their country as well as each government entity in detail. Mobile strategy implementations inevitably will face challenges stemming from these unique characters of each situation. mGovernment motivation mostly comes from citizens demand and as such they impose some unique requirements. Similar can be said for technological advances and the requirements imposed by them.

- **Plan for "Integration" and sharing resources**: Seeing the bigger picture also requires considerations in integration of the services and possible cooperation between government entities to create unique mobile services. Integrated services are the key development areas in mGovernment since it forms a fundamental base for comprehensive service development, which inturn comes out as one of the unique contribution of mobile government. Governments around the globe which realize they have missing elements in their strategic approach to mGovernment implementation are taking necessary steps to ensure they can provide integrated services that involve at least two or more government institutions or departments. Centralizing knowledge and databases, asset management and procurement databases, one point-access web services to all government applications are among these efforts to contribute to cooperation between different agencies. These efforts are valuable for the future of mGovernment projects but also result in immediate gains to reduce implementation and administration costs.

- **Build on existing structures**: Costs and feasibility are important factors in implementation of mGovernment services. As mobile technologies are evolving, governments should be in line with the evolution and make gradual amendments and investments on the existing systems and structures. Demolishing what is in hand and building brand new systems are too risky and may be costly. Also adoption of entirely new procedures and processes are far more difficult to implement and subject to a stronger organizational resistance most of the time. Therefore, making use of existing systems as much as possible in order to follow the evolving path of technology may be considered as a way to move forward. Governments should carefully analyze the potential of existing infrastructure in building the bricks of mGovernment and implement strategic steps of mGovernment fully.

- **Create collaboration between government organizations**: Most of the government services, in nature, require involvement of several agencies until they reach to the end users. In consequence, government institutions have constant interaction and communication with each other. With regard to mGovernment, it is not different and, as a result, the back-end cooperation between various government entities should be seamless and in harmony. This, however, is only possible by means of standardization of inter-connected processes such as data entry, data exchange and storage as well as security of sensitive data. When each entity keeps its own ways of processing data, collaboration between agencies becomes troublesome and inefficient to say the least. Common systems, software and security mechanisms are 'a must' in integrated mGovernment service architecture. Therefore, mGovernment strategy has to focus on potential collaboration areas and actions should be undertaken accordingly.[xviii]

- **Align legal base with the mGovernment strategy**: mGovernment transformation is a continuous process and will never be a finished project. With every new innovation in government service areas, there will be legal and regulatory conflicts that need to be resolved in line with new applications.[xix] Major services that need legal adjustments are those such as national mobile signature, mobileID, national mPayment services, etc. It is inevitable that these services bring new questions to be answered as to accountability, security and liability issues surrounding them. Therefore, cooperation with legal authorities on potential regulatory adjustments should be carried out on a continuous basis.

- **Seek mutually beneficial public private partnerships**: mGovernment implementation and its maintenance is not a procedure that can solely be managed by governments and local authorities alone. Involvement of all the relevant actors in the mobile value chain is the leading success factor for mGovernment. Governments' mGovernment strategies should set institutional arrangements in order to constantly keep close contact with private sector and citizens and businesses so that dynamic and mutually beneficial partnerships are settled with relatively easy and efficient collaboration of key stakeholders and are always sustained at all stages of the mGovernment transformation.[xx]

4. Prerequisites of mGovernment Implementation

mGovernment implementation has a number of prerequisites to be fulfilled to get things under way. This chapter discusses the initial steps of mGovernment implementation strategy such as the analysis of the country and citizens' profiles, existence of a strong leadership, guidance for government institutions in the mGovernment transition process and the capacity building at all levels.

4.1. Analyzing country specific context and citizen demand

There are specific organizational, social and economic structures as well as accompanying cultural values and tendencies that define each country's uniqueness. Nations have diverging budgets, infrastructural capacity, governing models and legal base. mGovernment strategies, services and applications vary depending on spatial, economic and social circumstances. Each case shows different characters in developing countries than in developed nations. Prerequisites differ from one economy to another due to existing infrastructure and social habits in any given territory. Technology trends, government approaches and citizen uptake are all subject to local circumstances. Managers of the mGovernment implementation should study and analyze the requirements of the peculiar conditions of their locality and then plan the entire procedure.

An analysis of the citizens' behavior also is crucial for predicting the demand for services. Citizens' utilization of technology, more often, goes ahead of stringent governmental institutions. For that reason governments should thoroughly analyze what the current technology usage among citizens suggests for government services. A well-rounded research of public preferences of mobile technology, how different communities use varying devices and measurement of general capabilities needs to be conducted and analyzed by policy makers. Citizens are definitely the ultimate targets of any given government service, thus, public demand is essentially the most crucial element influencing key decisions in mGovernment transformation.

4.2. Setting up a leadership to manage to mGovernment

A strong leadership and visionary unit is critical for setting achievable goals, analyzing existing opportunities and resources, planning strategic milestones for implementation, initiating executions of plans and policies, monitoring and evaluating project achievements on a regular basis and guiding each and every stakeholder for the same strategic goals.

Nature of some strategic decisions in mGovernment implementation leads normally to a central top-down decision processes. One dimension of this is related to implemention enabling infrastructure and services for other mGovernment services to integrate into. For instance, nationwide mobile payment infrastructure that forms as a base to other transactional services is a task that requires a central initiative. Similarly, implementing a government wide data center that would establish a network between all government entities cannot be implemented by local individual efforts. mobileID services, mobile financial services, implementation of nationwide TSMs are tasks that require central policy makers' leadership and initiative to be realized.[xxi]

mGovernment implementation requires effective engagement of different organizational partners in mGovernment ecosystem. Directing all the main stakeholders towards mGovernment project and building the entire management system is one of the most demanding challenge ahead. A lack of balanced combination of central top-down management and a local bottom-up decision-making process will make the implementation fail in variety of aspects.

In case of lacking central planning and leadership, mGovernment project most probably will suffer from standalone services that have no connection with other related government entities resulting in duplicate efforts. Failure in taking advantage of economies of scale will inevitably push up the costs. Eventually, potential strength of mobile technologies in public services will not be utilized efficiently, thus the integration of government services on mobile platform will be far from satisfactory.

Equally, to achieve a smartly implemented mGovernment services, top decision makers will require contribution and collaboration of local partners to comprehend the local climate and the required services. In the absence of bottom-up decision-making processes, the project will fail to benefit from involvement of citizens in creation and design of mobile services. In addition, the adoption of mGovernment services will substantially be lower than desired. A unifying strategic approach that embraces both top-down and bottom-up processes will create a network structure in which all government entities share resources and work together around the same goal.

4.3. Develop clear instructions for institutions

Government entities should be inline with the overall strategic approach of the whole mGovernment implementation. It is very critical to guide each involving agency into a collaborative path in harmony with other entities. Governments should have well-defined plans and detailed objectives for the transformation towards mGovernment and let every government agency have an understanding of these details.[xxii] Government institutions should also be directed as to what they might expect from this transformation and what preparations ought to be undertaken. Concise directives should be created and presented to all central and local government entities on mobile services, security issues, mobile device management (MDM) and mobile application management (MAM) principles as well as the general mobile services architecture. Institutions should also be assisted towards integrated services and shown clearly how to share responsibilities and workload when they provide services in cooperation with other government departments.[xxiii]

4.4. Start building capacity

It is not possible to express sufficiently the significance and importance of building capacity everywhere relevant is in making strategic implementations. Capacity building makes organizations fit to the understanding, development and deployment of mGovernment services. If this is ignored the implementation will be limping somewhere, slowing down and consuming the overall efforts drastically. Capacity building is relevant everywhere from technological to organizational and to the employees. It is also important to build capacity of the users in many countries, but the sections below focuses on public sector improvements, namely infrastructure, organizational and employee capacity building.

4.4.1. Infrastructure investments

In the process of transition to mGovernment, existing technological infrastructure will necessarily be enhanced and new investments should take place. It should be taken into account that infrastructure requirements in public services will be ongoing as long as there are new technological developments, therefore infrastructure setup and choice of technology should be considered with a solid future vision.[xxiv]

Studying the technological readiness of the country provides plenty of tips to understand what needs to be improved. There are two things to consider here: first technological readiness of the public sector and the second is technological readiness of the users. First one is related to the countrywide existing infrastructure i.e. mobile broadband, mobile network, data management architecture, Wi-Fi hotspots, etc. The second one is related to end users' access to technology. It is important to thoroughly study the mobile penetration rates, smart phone usage as well as consumer behavior towards mobile technology and services in order to design demand driven services that are accessible and usable.

While investing in infrastructure and new technology, the most visionary act is to plan for interoperability. Government services inevitably involve elements that require different bodies within its ecosystem to communicate with each other, exchange data, and take collaborative actions together. In order to attain an advanced level in mGovernment and provide integrated services to citizens, technology and infrastructure deployments must be handled with interoperability principles.[xxv]

4.4.2. Organizational Transformation

mGovernment will require some institutional rearrangements and potential new work definitions. Some positions will be redundant whereas some others will require new skills among the employees. New business processes will emerge with the involvement of mobile technology. Organizations should respond to the requirements of this transition as seamlessly as they can.[xxvi] There will also be a necessity to establish new departments as well as entirely new organizations to be able to proceed to an advanced mGovernment state (i.e. TSM, Innovation Centers, etc.).

The new style of working such as flexible working and bring your own device (BYOD) will be more prominent and acceptable. Public organization would see the benefits and make all necessary efforts to accommodate these where ever is possible. Adoption of such novel ways of working will strengthen the public sector organizations to cope with serious requirements of implementing strategic mGovernment.

4.4.3. Employee Capacity

Employees of public sector organization may often find it difficult to catch up with advances in new technologies and how they can be utilized in their work. Training plays an important role in government employee's capacity. Often there are requirements for a certain measure of technical capacity and knowledge relevant to mGovernment services. Both on the demand and supply side of the equation, improvements should be taken into consideration wherever deemed necessary. Government officers and workers should be familiarized with the new implementation specifications, and instructed towards the best practices that the mobile technology involved will require.[xxvii]

Civil workers may need to acquire new skills such as learning how to use a new wireless device or how to enter information via wireless networks. Although these devices and applications may be user friendly, depending on the age and background of the users, adaptation may take longer than anticipated, hindering the success of the project or causing delays in outcomes. Clear guidelines should be provided to government employees of all levels regarding their operational tasks and roles as well as about the related security and other technical matters. Organizational learning should be maintained continuously with trainings, staff education sessions and seminars, etc. Employees should also consider providing trainings to the citizens online or offline. Citizens should be able to use the services irrespective of their previous levels of capacity. Community groups should be given necessary support and assistance by the government if they lack any kind of technical knowledge or skills to use a service.

5. Where and How to Start?

This chapter addresses the essential primary steps of mGovernment implementation. The first section focuses on the eGovernment services that can be transferred to mGovernment. Second section elaborates on the ideas on how to prioritize the initial mGovernment services. In the last section, four systematic ways of offering mGovernment services are analyzed.

5.1. Evaluate existing eGov efforts potentially usable in mGov

Adopting new technology and developing new infrastructure is a costly investment. Reorganizing the workflow and business procedures adds additional costs to this investment. Therefore, when the adoption of technology is transforming the infrastructure and workflow from scratch it may involve huge risks. Among these risks, for example, are:

- technology may not be suitable for the service,
- systems may not be sufficiently secure, n
- ew systems may not work well with other existing services and make it difficult to integrate, etc.

 Instead of taking such high risks, policy makers should first consider what elements in the existing architecture could be used as a base for future services of mGovernment. Building on existing infrastructure not only provides cost minimization but also eases transitional stages of organizational restructuring. Hence, rather than a revolution in infrastructure and workflow, it might be the best to introduce gradual building on existing systems.

eGovernment transformation has been through various challenges and obstacles on the way systems are built for the use of government agencies, which are now integral part of the business processes in many countries. These gains of eGovernment generally provide good basis for mGovernment implementations.[xxviii] Consequently, every new mGovernment project should carefully analyze what given infrastructure suits to the future mGovernment services.

5.2. Prioritizing mGovernment Services

Determining priority developments in mGovernment implementation is a vital step. There are two areas of consideration when prioritizing. First is to evaluate the existing eGovernment services that are applicable to mobile platform, and second is to prioritize the service areas that *unique* and novel mGovernment services can be created.

5.2.1. eGovernment Service Conversion to mGovernment

As discussed in the previous section, it is convenient to start with the existing systems and migrate eGovernment services to mobile platform. Firstly, implementation managers should identify which of the eGovernment services are applicable as a mobile service in nature. Then the options should carefully be analyzed if these conversions would provide added value to the public services in terms of efficiency and costs. Popularity of the eGovernment service is a determining factor in this. Citizens' view should be observed by surveys in order to predict the demand for the mobile service.

Project managers should also consider potentials of revenue generation through migrated services, if any. A thorough investigation concerned with these questions would yield a set of eGovernment services that would be the best fit to migrate to mobile platform.[xxix]

5.2.2. Prioritizing Unique mGovernment Service Creation

Apart from direct conversion from eGovernment services, policy makers should investigate what the existing infrastructure can offer in terms of unique mobile services. A study of feasibility, public demand, potential added value analysis and applicability would present some results that can be provided as standalone mobile services. Among these, location based information services, notification applications and SMS based services would be a good starting point as initial developments in mGovernment implementation. Consequently, policymakers can focus more on integrated mobile services, which are more complex yet, offer more benefits.

5.3. Four systematic ways for Transition to mGovernment

Transformative impact of mobile technologies differs in government services due to different technology requirements of the back-end internal operations and front-end administration and public interactions. An overview of the approaches that transform different types of public services is discussed below.

5.3.1. Direct Conversion of eGovernment Services

Existing eGovernment applications can be made available to mobile users in various ways. Building on existing systems will be a better starting point than creating a brand new system since it provides database and statistics of adoption and acceptance of its users bringing about low investment and quick wins for both governments and citizens. One way of doing this is to convert the web services to mobile friendly formats. Depending on the screen size or the operating system, responsive designs display the content according to the device they are connecting to the service they use, so the user experience is not being disturbed using different devices.

Second way is to create native mobile applications from existing eGovernment services for several operating systems (iOS, Android, Blackberry). Rather than converting the whole website into mobile friendly format, these applications make use of the certain functions of the website available for the use of the applications for online or offline access. These applications vary from information search applications (i.e. nearest hospital, criminal laws, tourist guides) to more interactive applications such as mobile voting, surveys, event search, etc.

5.3.2. Empowering Mobile Workers in the Fields

Mobile workers are government employees whose jobs are outside the offices in the field such as inspection workers, emergency service, etc. A major role of mGovernment in this case is to transform the government entity into a well-connected entity by providing an integrated back-office infrastructure. Some of these include:

- security services (law enforcement, citizen security)
- inspection services of local authorities
- emergency and disaster management
- access to records remotely (public safety, health and education, etc.)

Some of these need to use real-time mobile access as seen in current mapping and planning technology, and traffic information systems. Emergency professionals extensively use VoIP systems, and various forms of PDAs are helping field workers to stay in touch with the office, and collaborate and work on the same document with other workers. For example, in the case with Police Force, using tablets, an authorized access to government database about criminal records, and in case of health workers, citizens' health history and ID information are provided.[xxx]

5.3.3. Flexible Working

These technologies are similar to those used by mobile workers but are for employees using mobile technologies to work from home or from any desk (a hot desk) in the office. The technologies for flexible working enforce mobile devices and applications that allow management of flexible work and employees from monitoring movements, scheduling to collaboration and access to government data. "Bring your own device" (BYOD) or "Choose your own device" (CYOD) concepts are starting to transform the working environment in business world and it will not last long before governments have to follow the suit with the new trend.[xxxi]

5.3.4. Unique Citizen Centric Mobile Services

There are then other services that are unique to mGovernment (not possible in eGovernment) and are directed to citizens. This privilege is brought by mobile technologies and can allow citizens to access services any and anywhere. Driving in an out of parking space and paying your ticket automatically via sensors is a good example of such applications.

Citizen centric mobile services are intended to extend governments' reach to its citizens in a more effective way and to make government services available at all times and to be able to share data and information with users wherever they are. Using these technologies, users may access current government information, make transactions and payments, log their tax returns, give feedback, make appointments, vote or make a request, register and report.

6. Implementing Key Enablers

At the center of implementing strategic mobile government is making sure fundemantal building blocks are in place within a country. We call these key enablers. Here in this section we will discuss major key enablers for the implementation of a progressive mGovernment :

- mobileID,
- Data Centers,
- Trusted Service Manager,
- Mobile Payment and
- Government App Portal.

Implementing these key enablers opens up an endless territory for innovative and integrated mGovernment solutions that transform our daily lives. A strategic approach to mGovernment implementation should always consider setting up these key enablers, however, we should note that these require advanced technical and organizational robustness within the applied context, and not all the countries currently are capable of implementing all of these as a first step to mGovernment due to limited resources and other reasons.

Key Enablers of mGovernment

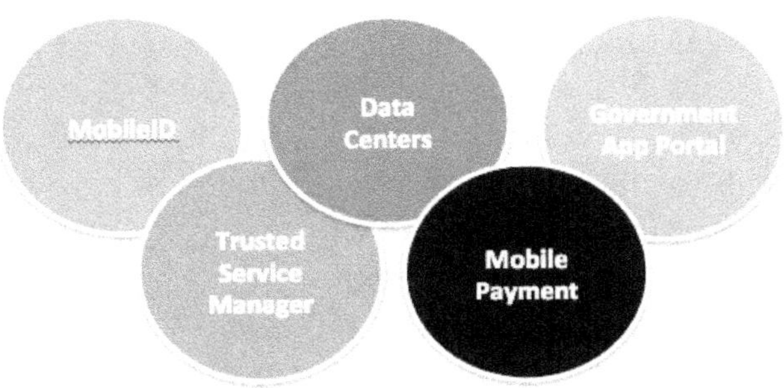

Figure 2. Key Enablers of mGovernment

6.1. mobileID

A Nationwide mobileID system is a key enabler that can provide privacy and authentication security in mobile transactions through various types of authentication and authorization mechanisms. It is, without a doubt, one of the prominent foundation stones of mGovernment. Once established, mobileID opens up new paths to endless number of mobile services from Near Field Communication (NFC) payments to banking transactions; toll payments to e-participation as well as many other possibilities in mHealth, mEducation and mTransport. However, setting up a nationwide mobileID scheme across the country is a very complex task that requires cooperation between several stakeholders. Still it is not sufficient to achieve a successful implementation unless mobileID is used by citizens with absolute confidence regarding their security and privacy.

Several pioneer countries successfully experimented with national Electronic IDs and mobileID projects such as Belgium, France, Norway, Oman, Estonia, Finland, Turkey and recently United Arab Emirates. The adoption rates are still not anywhere near its inevitable potential however the experiences from these countries indicate a lot about the future of mobileID. [xxxii]

Estonia is one of the early adopters of mobileID and Estonians can interact with more than 400 government and business services ranging from electronic banking to switching pension funds, to applying for a driver's license through Mobile Identification. [xxxiii]

Inherently, Mobile Identification enables end users to authenticate and identify themselves through Mobile Network Operators (MNO)s without revealing their private data to the service providers. Authentication may be ensured by one of the following ways[xxxiv]:
- User name and password authentication
- Phone Number authentication
- Simple one time password (OTP)
- Mobile PKI solution (Public Key Infrastructure)
- Smart Card NFC (Near Field Communication)

mobileID depending on the nature of its implementation involves several stakeholders including central and local government bodies, MNOs, service providers and, in some cases, financial institutions all of which have unique contributions and concrete interests.

6.2. Data Centers & Integration

Perhaps this is one of the most challenging requirements for the strategic mGovernment to reach its aspired goals. We are living in the age of so called "Big Data". Data collection and data management are proving to be the key challenge and at the same time a strategic opportunity to governments and businesses. There is a vast amount of data available to public sector and ongoing developments to add even more by new channels of information with new technologies. Being able to turn these huge data sets into meaningful tools in order to divert policies, allocate resources, invest in inadequate operations and bring in new services is a magical power at the hands of governments. This means that governments can have deeper insights, establish evidence based decision-making procedures, create to-the-point services as long as they can make effective use of the "Big Data".[xxxv]

There are various challenges that need to be tackled when implementing a data handling strategy regarding infrastructure building; security, standardization and interoperability issues; system, data and service integration between different entities; and usability and reusability of the datasets and acquired information; and limited accessibility of information.

In order to overcome these challenges, data strategies should involve policies to promote data standards to avoid duplicate data creation efforts and to attain reusability of the data by other parties involved so that interoperability would be achieved within the network of government entities as well as with citizens and businesses.[xxxvi] Establishing a nationwide Data Centre may present a solid base for mGovernment development by facilitating interoperability, increasing cooperation between government agencies and bring in a more integrated approach in mGovernment service creation.

Usually, every government entity holds great deal of public data in its own database and much of these data is duplicate of the other institutions' data. However, in cases where there is a network of public data communication across government institutions, the efforts to keep track of the information and the costs diminish dramatically. It is important to manage the data categorically with a taxonomical hierarchy so that the "Big Data" turns into a huge resource that relevant data can be derived in a meaningful way, and moreover, it could be used and re-used by other authorized bodies as well.

Data integration, however difficult to realize, enables governments to transform huge data sets to be organized, and categorical information; to open public data for citizens and businesses for better transparency, to reduce duplicate efforts to create and manage data; and to provide integrated services by a better network of data flow and cooperation between government entities.[xxxvii]

Without proper data integration and permitted use by vaious government entities it is impossible to offer advanced services to citizens where government operates seamlessly and provides convenient and useful services. Imagine the value of cooperation that may exist among emergency services in the case of fire and accident where several citizens are involved.

6.3. Trusted Service Manager (TSM)

A TSM is an independently acting body to manage and secure transactions made by mediating the transactional process between customers (mobile device users), service providers and MNOs. NFC technology has been around for a while to enable payments with mobile devices. However managing the transaction with advanced authorization and security is a more complex task that involves some technical sophistications that needs to be in place by engaging stakeholders. TSM, as a service security management entity, handles these technical and contractual complications between involved parties in the transaction.[xxxviii]

We see that the role is central to leveraging the benefits of secure mobile transactions. TSM is the trusted entity to enable the transactions without any interference to the business aspect relationships between service providers, MNOs, the citizens, financial institutions and software developers. Apart from securing transactions, the functions of TSM are setting contractual agreements with the parties involved; handling customer relations for TSM activities; managing secure element lifecycle and service lifecycles; testing and evaluating new services and setting standards for eligibility; and administrative tasks such as billing and reporting.[xxxix]

The question arises as to who exactly will be playing the TSM role in the marketplace and what sort of business model should be pursued. It is meant to be a trusted third party (TTP) to mediate the complex relationship between involved actors. It is in the very core center of the mobile payment business so it is a role that many stakeholders are willing to play. The argument about which actors in the mobile value chain are the best candidates to take over this role such as MNOs, card associations and banks has all been discussed as to whether they would be capable to act as a TTP. For a universal solution with the most adoptability potential, however, a more neutrally managed independent TSM settings seem to be the most sustainable solution rather than one or two stakeholders in the market mediating as the TTP. Therefore, it is essential to set up a neutral TSM of whose key tasks and responsibilities are shared among the market actors who are the most capable of providing the service and cooperate to increase the potential of mobile payment technology without fragmenting the market.[xl]

Governments should ideally have no more than a leading role to initiate the cooperation between these stakeholders to operate together in order to enable secure mobile transactions. This will open up paths to new service creation, increase the trust to use mobile devices for transactions and expand the mobile market to new possibilities. A neutral TSM, as markets mature, may even provide additional services in healthcare, mobile signature, transport ticketing and mobile voting etc. as long as it would establish itself as an independent, widespread and trusted party.

6.4. Mobile Payment (mPayment)

At the heart of most monetary transactional mGovernment services lies a secure payment system using mobile and wireless technologies. mPayment is used to describe transactions that a mobile device is used to initiate and confirm a payment to purchase services or goods. There are various types of mPayment methods that are currently in use to pay for digital commodities (i.e. e-books, music, software and apps, etc.) as well as physical items.[xli] Mobile commerce is a growing domain in markets and governments are also initiating mPayment schemes in public services. There are a great number of application areas where citizens can perform transactions via a mobile device such as paying for taxes, utility bills, visa and passport fees, parking and road toll fees, transport tickets, tuition fees, medical pharmaceutical costs, etc.[xlii]

Technologies used in mPayment depend on the infrastructure and the nature of the payment as well. It ranges from SMS payments to NFC payments. MNOs generally are at the heart of the mPayment facilities to mediate between consumers and service providers by providing the infrastructure and network. Other intermediaries, for instance financial institutions, can also facilitate mPayment that enable credit card based payments, or specialist transfer companies like PayPal or BPay using service applications, etc. [xliii]

To enable mPayment systems in the public sector and in the industry securely, however, there are diversified issues to solve. Firstly, there is a legal base to settle in order to define the rules and accountabilities of the usage of mobile devices in transactions. More importantly, the security and privacy of end users should be a priority policy to implement. Interoperability is also a key concern to maintain since payment systems should comply with all types of mobile devices, be valid through all the MNOs and work for all financial institutions. A national mPayment architecture should be designed so that the systems are deeply integrated and highly secure.

6.5. Government Apps Portal

There is need for a platform that enables citizens to access to the services developed via mGovernment and developing such a medium requires serious considerations.

Government institutions in local and central level provide some of their mGovernment services through native mobile applications to end-users. Mobile services such as nearest pharmacy search, doctor appointment and notification apps, location based tourist information services, mobile payment services, government field workers software apps etc. are being used by several different components of the government. The idea behind a Government App Store, however, is to gather citizen centric services provided by different government institutions to one single point of access web portal to increase awareness about the services and promote their adoption.[xliv] Furthermore, government apps portals can also be managed in a way that enhances the strategic cooperation between agencies to create integrated and innovative mobile services by setting application standards; testing and evaluating new services; guiding service developers through security and usability issues; and providing consultancy to local and central government entities to improve their mobile presence.[xlv]

Initiating a government app portal encourages cost efficient service application development towards citizens and government employees, avoids duplicate efforts that might occur, and raises awareness concerning the existing services among government institutions and citizens. Moreover, these portals can be used to promote innovative service development by awarded calls for service creation. Also they can utilize a forum? that the past experiences of application developers that would guide new initiatives.

7. Promoting Adoption of mGovernment Services

mGovernment implementation has more to do with assurances of user uptake than just building infrastructure, setting up enablers and creating mobile services. Reaching out to end users and gaining acceptance is the a crucial element of any successful IT project. In mGovernment context, these are citizen adoption of the provided services, adoption by government entities and employees, and finally a wider deployment of the provided services.

This chapter analyses the factors affecting citizens' uptake of the offered mobile services. The same issue is also investigated for the government entities and employees. Subsequently, this chapter clarifies what the best strategy would be for wider deployment of the initial services and the key role the pilot projects play in spreading small-scale mGovernment services to widespread implementations.

Adoption of mGovernment has certain barriers on both the citizens' side and the government entities' side. These barriers vary from cultural structures to technical capacities and from lack of awareness to resistance to change. Thus, planning an efficient campaign to raise awareness and engage users, is as crucial as developing the mobile services.

7.1. Promoting mGovernment to Citizens

Attracting citizens' attention and intelligent campaigns are important factors in adoption of services. Past experience demonstrates that many innovative mGovernment services have fallen short of initial expectations in terms of adoption rates due to the lack of public awareness. Government strategists do not always regard the advocacy and promotion campaigns as the most important element in mGovernment service implementation but in fact it is a vital step in the process. Without people using the designed service, mGovernment services are mere waste of public resources because the main motive is to reach out to citizens in various new channels via mobile technologies.

Governments and service providers should plan the promotional steps in service implementation ahead of time. Promotion and advocacy may take many forms depending on the context. Advertisements, notifications, billboards on public offices television spots are just a few of them. However, there is more that governments can do to promote their mobile services, for example, to engage citizens and businesses in the process of creation and design of the services. People are more inclined to using services that they actually took part or had a say in producing. By engaging users in the process, service providers take a giant step to design high quality services that address the exact requirements of the users.

From citizen's perspective, expecting them to take any mService offered quickly and in large numbers is often a very optimistic approach. While some citizens need simply to be notified about the services, the others may need more campaigning and support as they may be on the less privileged side of the digital divide where they may have difficulties in terms of accessibility and usability. Therefore, citizen adoption depends on a number of issues such as awareness, perceived convenience, security and privacy implications, usefulness of the applications and trust.[xlvi] Demonstrating potential benefits to the users and gaining their trust is as important as designing mobile services. Meeting and exceeding the expectations is the way to achieve citizen satisfaction from the services provided.

The most common issues raising doubts over mobile services are security and privacy issues.[xlvii] Citizens should be provided with strong assurance from trusted bodies that the data they share when using government services is safe in storage and exchange. An interoperable authentication system that citizens can use to access sensitive government services is the ultimate way forward in resolving trust issues and a very big challenge to overcome as implementing it requires several legal, infrastructural and organizational changes.

7.2. Promotions for Government Entities and Employees

Similar challenges exist in working environment, too. Government employees do not always embrace process and procedure rearrangements. When not properly informed about the new services they will serve, employees may even feel insecure and doubtful over the upcoming changes. As mGovernment requires a certain level of organizational restructuring and business process management, the workflow may necessarily be subject to change.[xlviii][xlix] It is very common to see resistance to change or reluctance to adopt the new ways of performing tasks. In order to eliminate potential resistance, employees should be given chances to see clear advantages of using mobile technologies.

As for the government employees' case, training and education of the employees is another crucial challenge to adopt mGovernment services in each evolutionary step of transition. Seminars, training lessons, practical teaching and service testing should take place to minimize service failures and visualize the benefits to the employees.[l] Communicating the actual benefits of the new technology to the government employees is highly necessary in order to gain user acceptance for technology adoption. When employees realize the benefits of the implemented service to their workflows resistance to change may diminish substantially.

7.3. Encouraging Pilot Projects for Wider Deployment

The transition to strategic mGovernment is not a straightforward leap to better governance. Even the most obvious and advanced developments require some testing and experience in order to explore the impact, feasibility, organizational requirements, adoption and usability of the services. Pilot projects provide a great deal of useful observations that may help refining the eventual roll out phase of the entire implementation. This is why piloting is an essential part of most implementation projects and equally is working with small-scale experiments with a focus on a widespread deployment.[li]

In mGovernment pilot projects, planners may investigate several issues such as the adequacy of infrastructure, applicability in real life conditions, cost & benefit of the project, the level of cooperation required among the service providers, unforeseen results, user acceptance and adoption potential. These observations play a significant role in scaling up the pilot project to a wider area of usage. Promising pilot projects often end up successfully when implemented in bigger scale and more importantly inspire other similar projects in other cities and countries enabling mGovernment projects to be adopted by a wider base.

The effectiveness of pilot projects also depends on the opportunities to engage users in evaluating the planned implementation, hence increasing the chances for a widespread adoption of mobile services. Testing a mobile service with end users may provide insights to the expectations of the target audience. The same is applicable to government institutions and employees. Early pilot applications and services prove to be useful for innovative mobile services since they let the project managers spot what institutional arrangements work the best in favor of providing the intended mobile services. Pilot programs also give employees an early chance to improve workflows and service quality by experiencing it beforehand, finding errors and drawbacks.

8. **Progressive mGovernment Implementation**

As mGovernment brings a whole new approach to public services, along with it comes big complications in institutional architecture, technology infrastructure, political support and determination, legal and policy issues and last but not the least citizen acceptance. Ideal direction that governments are seeking is to reach a stage of advanced mGovernment powered by cloud and the Internet of Things (IoT) where public service is ubiquitous, context-aware, efficiently integrated and straight to the point of need. Technological implications are showing glimpses of such a future however there are still gaps and challenges on the path to mGovernment because solely relying on technological advances without a collaborative effort to implement smart solutions to public service evidently will not go too far.

We should probably start with thinking what direction mobile technologies are following and what future mGovernment services are aimed by governments around the world.

Smartphone is strengthening the big influence on daily life along with innovative applications such IoT. Smartphone penetration rates have soared in recent years especially in developed nations. These devices have many additional features that service providers can utilize, namely: GPRS, Bluetooth, cameras with video capabilities, advanced web browsers, push notification systems, and other sensors, etc. Many mobile service providers utilize device features to design innovative applications that have not been possible with any other widely used technology. Some of them include mapping applications (city guides, nearest drugstore or police station searchers), reminders and notifications (medication reminders, school curriculums and deadlines notifications), NFC payment services, complaint-filing services with image support, etc.[lii]

Powerful hardware and content combination along with a content sharing platform is opening up possibilities of tailor made systems for use in healthcare, education, transportation and all sorts of public services. Trends in open source mobile operating systems and also trends in user interface, design screen size & capacity are all contributing to the evolution of the potential mobile services. HD video is becoming a powerful component of the smart phones; top-notch smart mobile devices are gradually having dual core processors increasing battery life and processing speed; 3D video technologies are being adapted to handsets.[liii]

Context-aware services are promising to be influencing the future of mGovernment. Mobile phones are increasingly getting equipped with features that allow sensing the context of the user. Bluetooth and GPRS features nowadays provide opportunities for new application and service design. Location based tourism services, traffic and weather update services as well as emergency management services that make use of device features are getting popular in developed countries.[liv]

Another trend among leading governments is the effort to personalize public services as best as they can. Personalized public services through mobile devices can also be studied under the topic of context-aware services.[lv] Governments of developed countries are recently showing efforts to utilize mobileID services in order to be used in several situations that need authentication such as accessing personal data, using in formal procedures during interaction with government offices and in some cases for mobile payments.

A big part of these efforts are consisting of bringing together key stakeholders around the same project and also to make necessary legal amendments for mobileID case. A strong political will is required to manage the relationships between a complex ecosystem of various stakeholders and security and privacy issues should be handled with trusted agencies in order to achieve success. However, mobileID services, once implemented, can pave the way for many useful services targeted directly to each individual. Tax bill payments, refund requests, accessing personal medical history and sharing with doctors and any other forms of service that proof of identity is required can be managed by authenticated mobile devices. Estonia has been one of the leading countries that legislated mobileID services which was built on existing electronic ID system in the country. Currently in United Arab Emirates, mobile network operators and government are working in collaboration to implement mobileID.[lvi]

Importance of "enabling" mGovernment infrastructure is very crucial as it is the case with mobileID. Enabling services are those that can be used for other modular extensions and are a base for new services innovation. Strategically oriented governments are taking these efforts and a collaborative action is being undertaken by all the key stakeholders for building the future of mGovernment. These infrastructure/services are:

- a nationwide mobile payment system that all mobile payment services can integrate; a mobileID system to authenticate and authorize mobile device users once and for all government services and transactions;
- Trusted Service Manager services in order to enable NFC payments;
- a shared database with set standards of data storage, exchange in order to realize a genuine integration between different agencies within the government network;
- a common security/privacy policy that is agreed between all agencies and stakeholders.

These are the core enablers on the path to the future of mGovernment services towards ubiquitous governments enhanced with new technologies. The path to advanced mGovernment, therefore, follows a track of several adjustments being made to legal and regulatory environment and at the same time infrastructural and organizational architectures. An analysis of the gaps between what is possible and what is the current state of mGovernment revolves around the existence of enabling infrastructure.

ABOUT mobileGov UK

mobileGov UK offers effective strategic consultancy services based on its influential activities in Mobile Government(TM) practice and approaches and leads mGov(TM) services to citizens in the EU and in countries such as Japan, UAE, Korea, Canada, Afghanistan and Turkey.

- Our company has been influencing many governments' strategies for mobile Government.
- Our company is the founder and the world leader of mGovernment Practice.
- Our company is the only organization having a comprehensive knowledge of history and current developments of International mGovernment Practice.
- Our company created and works with the largest and effective network of government organizations, international experts and other relevant stakeholders:
- Our company holds the only existing international conference on mobileGovernment and relevant conferences on mobile development and society (pleas see **www.m4life.org**):
- Our company builds upon years of experience in the mGovernment practice.

In short, Our company offers quality mGovernment advisory services based on its comprehensive knowledge of the field and other governments' experiences, the network of key expertise and ability conduct international training programs and seminars. For more feel free to visit: www.mgovernment.net.

Trademarks Licensing

mGov, mGovernment, mobileGov and mobileGovernment are trademarks of mobileGov UK. Unlicensed use is prohibited. Please write to ik@mgovernment.net or visit www.mgovernment.net for licensing or permissions

A Short Bio of Prof. I. Kushchu

Ibrahim Kushchu is the founder of the field of Mobile Government – the use of mobile technologies in the public sector to offer services to citizens. His expertise also cover community informatics, enterprise mobility, management systems and artificial intelligence. Combining his management studies and his expertise in artificial intelligence, Prof. Kushchu has been working for business schools in the UK and in Japan, and teaching various information communication technology courses especially related to ICT, electronic business and mobile business.

Prof. Kushchu is an internationally recognized pioneering practitioner and researcher in developing the mobile government field by bringing into the light the issues related to the use of mobile technologies in electronic government. His work also extends to impact of mobile technologies on economic and social development. He has developed strategies and road map for mobile government for various countries in the world including recent ones in Afghanistan and the United Arab Emirates.

In addition to working with governments, and he has been working with various multi-national organizations including GATES FOUNDATION, CISCO, NOKIA, HITACHI, and NTT DoCoMo at projects involving consultancy, research, and educational events. He also offers advisory services to local and central government organization and their agencies.

He has edited and co-edited three books and has a number of publications in various international journals and in the proceedings of reputable conferences. He is also very active in international community of researchers through speaking, organizing, chairing, co-chairing various international conferences, and serving in the committees.

Prof. Kushchu holds a first degree (BSc) in management. He also has an MBA and a Master's degree (MSc) in artificial intelligence from the University of Edinburgh, UK. He was awarded a PhD degree in evolutionary artificial intelligence from the University of Sussex, UK.

References

ⁱ Castells, Manuel, and Gustavo Cardoso. *The network society: From knowledge to policy.* Manuel Castells & Gustavo Cardoso. Center for Transatlantic Relations, Paul H. Nitze School of Advanced International Studies, Johns Hopkins University, 2006.

ⁱⁱ "The Global Information Technology Report 2015 - weforum.org ..." 2015. 29 Feb. 2016 <http://www3.weforum.org/docs/WEF_Global_IT_Report_2015.pdf>

ⁱⁱⁱ Kushchu, Ibrahim, and Halid Kuscu. "From E-government to M-government: Facing the Inevitable." *the 3rd European Conference on e-Government* 3 Jul. 2003: 253-260.

^{iv} Trimi, Silvana, and Hong Sheng. "Emerging trends in M-government." *Communications of the ACM* 51.5 (2008): 53-58.

^v "Information technology and learning: Their relationship and ..." 2015. 29 Feb. 2016 <https://webs.um.es/angelmer/miwiki/lib/exe/fetch.php?id=publicaciones&cache=cache&media=merono-_it_learning.pdf>

^{vi} "Need to know review number three: Local government in the ..." 2014. 29 Feb. 2016 <http://www.local.gov.uk/documents/10180/11515/Local+government+in+the+digital+age+(Need+to+know+Knowledge+Navigator+number+3)/544d1515-3483-4a58-8da4-da92eca6126b>

^{vii} Mofleh, Samer, Mohammed Wanous, and Peter Strachan. "Understanding national e-government: the role of central government." *Electronic Government, an International Journal* 6.1 (2009): 1-18.

^{viii} Lönn, CM. "An m-Government Solution for Complaint and ... - DiVA Portal." 2014. <https://www.diva-portal.org/smash/get/diva2:719075/FULLTEXT01.pdf>

^{ix} Foth, Marcus. *From social butterfly to engaged citizen: urban informatics, social media, ubiquitous computing, and mobile technology to support citizen engagement.* MIT Press, 2011.

^x Lasica, JD. "Civic Engagement on the Move: How mobile media can ..." 2008. <http://www.aspeninstitute.org/sites/default/files/content/docs/cands/Civic_Engagement_on_the_Move.pdf>

^{xi} "mobile Government Guidelines, by mobile Gov UK, 2015

^{xii} "A Point of View Paper from the GSMA." 2014. 29 Feb. 2016 <http://www.gsma.com/personaldata/wp-content/uploads/2012/08/GSMA-Mobile-Identity-Points-of-View-Report_FINAL.pdf>

^{xiii} Cox, C. "Trusted Service Manager: The Key to Accelerating Mobile ..." 2009. < https://www.firstdata.com/downloads/thought-leadership/fd_mobiletsm_whitepaper.pdf>

xiv Al-khamayseh, S. "Towards Citizen Centric Mobile Government Services: A ..." 2010. <http://unpan1.un.org/intradoc/groups/public/documents/apcity/unpan040048.pdf>

xv "Integrating Mobiles into Development Projects ... - USAID." 2015. 29 Feb. 2016 <https://www.usaid.gov/sites/default/files/documents/1861/M4DHandbook_August_2014.pdf>

xvi Wohltorf, J. "Decision Cockpit for Mobile Services - CiteSeer." 2015. <http://citeseerx.ist.psu.edu/viewdoc/download?doi=10.1.1.557.8325&rep=rep1&type=pdf>

xvii "e-Government Strategy 2014-2016 - الحكومة الالكترونية." 2013. 29 Feb. 2016 <http://www.jordan.gov.jo/wps/wcm/connect/cafec32b-3bf0-4fe0-af70-977ff8f6fbd4/e-Government+Strategy_Draft1.3.doc?MOD=AJPERES>

xviii "M – Government System Service Architecture ... – KAIST IITP." 2015. 29 Feb. 2016 <http://ittp.kaist.ac.kr/_prog/_board/common/download.php?code=mater_0402&ntt_no=270&atch_no=1>

xix McMillan, S. "Legal and Regulatory Frameworks for Mobile Government." 2012. <https://ofti.org/wp-content/uploads/2012/07/legal-and-regulatory-frameworks-for-moble-government.pdf>

xx "Gov2020: A Journey into the Future of Government - Deloitte." 2015. 29 Feb. 2016 <https://www2.deloitte.com/content/dam/Deloitte/au/Documents/public-sector/deloitte-au-ps-gov2020-journey-future-government2-130315.pdf>

xxi "mGovernment Roadmap of the UAE" 2013 by mobileGov UK.

xxii "E-Government Strategic Action Plan for the Public Service of ..." 2014. 29 Feb. 2016 <http://www.gov.na/documents/10181/18040/e-Gov+Strategic+Plan+for+the+Public+Service+2014+to+2018/cce8facc-309d-43cd-ab3d-e5ce714eaf69>

xxiii "IBM MobileFirst in Action for mGovernment and Citizen ..." 2015. 29 Feb. 2016 <http://www.redbooks.ibm.com/redpapers/pdfs/redp5168.pdf>

xxiv Justman, Moshe, and Morris Teubal. "Technological infrastructure policy (TIP): creating capabilities and building markets." *Technological Infrastructure Policy* (1996): 21-58.

xxv "e-Government and New Technologies - Public ..." 2015. 29 Feb. 2016 <https://publicadministration.un.org/publications/content/PDFs/E-Library%20Archives/2011%20EGM_e-Goverment%20and%20New%20Technologies.pdf>

xxvi Georgescu, M. "15 THE IMPACT OF MOBILE GOVERNMENT IN ..." 2011. <http://seap.usv.ro/annals/ojs/index.php/annals/article/viewFile/276/284>

xxvii Goldstein, KM. "Chapter 6 - World Bank Internet Error Page AutoRedirect." 2012. <http://siteresources.worldbank.org/EXTINFORMATIONANDCOMMUNICATIONAN DTECHNOLOGIES/Resources/IC4D-2012-Chapter-6.pdf>

xxviii Wicander, G. "Mobile Supported e-Government Systems - Simple search." 2011. <http://kau.diva-portal.org/smash/get/diva2:447593/FULLTEXT01.pdf>

xxix "FROM eGOVERNMENT TO MOBILE GOVERNMENT." Kushchu and Kuscu, 2003

xxx Gouscos, D. "A Proposed Architecture For Mobile Government - CiteSeer." 2009. <http://citeseerx.ist.psu.edu/viewdoc/download?doi=10.1.1.97.7670&rep=rep1&type=pdf >

xxxi "Top 2013 Trends for State and Local Government." 2013. 29 Feb. 2016 <http://www.govdelivery.com/pdfs/WP_2013_trends_slt.pdf>

xxxii "National MobileID schemes (Volume I) - Cryptome." 2015. <https://cryptome.org/2015/02/gemalto-gov-national-mobile-id.pdf>

xxxiii "Mobile Identity - Unlocking the Potential of the ... - GSMA." 2014. <http://www.gsma.com/personaldata/wp-content/uploads/2014/10/14-10-10-GSMA-SIA-Joint-Paper-Mobile-Identity_October-2014.pdf>

xxxiv "Downloaded from..." 2014. <http://www.id.gov.ae/assets/VIkVTCns.pdf.aspx>

xxxv Ubaldi, B. "Open Government Data - Open Data Forum." 2013. <http://www.opendataforum.info/files/OECD_Barbara_Ubaldi.pdf>

xxxvi "Discussion - Roadmap for digital government - Montgomery ..." 2012. 29 Feb. 2016 <http://www.montgomerycountymd.gov/content/council/pdf/agenda/cm/2012/121126/20 121126_GO1.pdf>

xxxvii "4. Big Data - Infocomm Development Authority of Singapore." 2012. 29 Feb. 2016 <https://www.ida.gov.sg/~/media/Files/Infocomm%20Landscape/Technology/Technolog yRoadmap/BigData.pdf>

xxxviii "The Role of the Trusted Service Manager in Mobile ... - GSMA." 2014. 29 Feb. 2016 <http://www.gsma.com/digitalcommerce/wp-content/uploads/2013/12/GSMA-TSM-White-Paper-FINAL-DEC-2013.pdf>

xxxix "NFC: The role of TSM Trusted Service Manager - Gemalto." 2014. 29 Feb. 2016 <http://www.gemalto.com/techno/inspired/nfc/tsm>

xl "Business models for NFC payments - Institut für ..." 2012. 29 Feb. 2016 <http://www.sicherungssysteme.net/fileadmin/Mobey_Forum_White_Paper_Business_m odels_for_NFC_payments.pdf>

xli Soni, A. "M-Payment Between Banks Using SMS - IEEE Xplore." 2010. <http://ieeexplore.ieee.org/iel5/5/5466592/05466601.pdf?arnumber=5466601>

xlii Ahsan, A. "Community Perception of Mobile Payment in e ... - DRO." 2012. <https://dro.deakin.edu.au/eserv/DU:30049159/ahsan-communityperception-2012.pdf>

xliii Ahsan, A. "Community Perception of Mobile Payment in e ... - DRO." 2012. <https://dro.deakin.edu.au/eserv/DU:30049159/ahsan-communityperception-2012.pdf>

xliv "Adoption of mGovernment service initiative in developing ..." 2015. 1 Mar. 2016 <https://www.researchgate.net/publication/279848235_Adoption_of_mGovernment_serv ice_initiative_in_developing_countries_A_citizen-centric_public_service_delivery_perspective_19th_ITS_Biennial_Conference_2012_Ban gkok_Thailand_18_-_21_November_2012_Moving>

xlv "mGovernment Roadmap." 2013 by mobileGov UK. 29 Feb. 2016

xlvi Abdelghaffar, H. "The Adoption of Mobile Government Services in Developing ..." 2012. <http://esjournals.org/journaloftechnology/archive/vol2no4/vol2no4_1.pdf>

xlvii Al-Khamayseh, Shadi, Elaine Lawrence, and Agnieszka Zmijewska. "Towards understanding success factors in interactive mobile government." *the Proceedings of Euro mGov* 2006.
xlviii

xlix "Managing Change and Innovation in Government - Springer." 2013. 1 Mar. 2016 <http://link.springer.com/content/pdf/10.1007%2F978-1-4419-1506-1_6.pdf>

l Ibrahim Kushchu. "Mobile government and organizational effectiveness." *Proceedings of the First European Conference on Mobile Government, Brighton, UK: Mobile Government Consortium* Jul. 2005: 56-66.

li World Health Organization. "Beginning with the end in mind: planning pilot projects and other programmatic research for successful scaling up." (2011).

lii Eom, Seok-Jin, and Jun Houng Kim. "The adoption of public smartphone applications in Korea: Empirical analysis on maturity level and influential factors." *Government Information Quarterly* 31 (2014): S26-S36.

liii "Chapter 5 Technology Options For mobile Solutions - ITU." 2012. 1 Mar. 2016 <https://www.itu.int/ITU-D/cyb/app/docs/m-gov/Technology%20options%20for%20mobile%20solutions.pdf>

liv Mukherjee, A. "Simple Implementation Framework for m-Government ..." 2005. <http://dl.acm.org/citation.cfm?id=1084228>

lv "Chapter 5 - Public Administration and Development ..." 2015. 1 Mar. 2016 <https://publicadministration.un.org/egovkb/Portals/egovkb/Documents/un/2014-Survey/Chapter5.pdf>

lvi "mGovernment Roadmap." 2013. mobileGov UK1 Mar. 2016 <

www.ingramcontent.com/pod-product-compliance
Lightning Source LLC
Chambersburg PA
CBHW051009050726
47592CB00007B/2766